AMERICA: A Dream

by Stanford Makishi
illustrated by José Miralles

AMERICA: A Dream

by Stanford Makishi
illustrated by José Miralles

Strategy Focus

Jiro Akamine came to America with a big dream. As you read, stop every now and then to **summarize** each part of the story.

In the late 1800s, people from all over the world were coming to California. They all had a dream of a better life in America. Some of these people, mostly men, came from Japan. This story is about one man, Jiro Akamine. His story is made up from the true stories of many different Japanese men. If Akamine had really lived, he would have told this story when he was a very old man in the 1960s.

My family in Japan did not have much money, but we were happy. Our small farm gave us enough to eat. I had many friends. Most of all, I was proud to work with my mother and father on the farm.

As I got older, though, I wanted more for my family. I thought that if I could get an education, I might be able to have a good job someday.

By the time I turned 14, I knew that I would not get the education that I wanted if I stayed in Niigata. I had a cousin and some friends who had gone to find jobs and go to school in California in America.

I made my decision. I would go to America too.

I came to America with one big dream. My dream was to have a good education. No one in my family had finished school, and I wanted to be the first to do it.

Like some other Japanese people who came to America, my plan was to learn to speak English. I wanted to finish school in America and then go back to Japan. Then, I thought, I could find a good job in my homeland. I was not the only one with this dream.

I came to California in 1885. I had been on a boat from Japan for days and days. Here I was, finally, in San Francisco.

When I walked off the boat, I realized that I would not return to Japan for a very, very long time. I thought about my family in Niigata. For a moment, I had the terrible thought that I might never return to them.

I didn't really know where to go. But that night, I found my way to a rooming house on Golden Gate Avenue. One of my cousins had told me I might rent a cheap room there.

"Hello, my name is Jiro Akamine," I said to the large man in charge. "I would like to rent a room here." I checked the American coins in my hand. My cousin had sent them to me in Japan. "I have only sixty cents," I said.

Luckily, the large man spoke Japanese. He answered, "We rent rooms for fifteen cents per night. Meals are thirty cents per day."

I thought for a while. I figured out that I could stay there for four nights with the money I had, if I did not pay for meals. I finally said, "Yes, I would like to rent a room for four nights."

"Okay," the man said. "That will be sixty cents, please." I gave him all the money I had.

"Let me show you to your room," the man said with a kind smile.

As we walked up a flight of stairs and then down a dark hallway, I thought about what I had done. I had a place to stay for four nights, but I didn't know how I would eat. I was scared.

I wondered if I had made a mistake in coming to America. I had no money now, and of course I didn't have a job. I spoke only Japanese. When I arrived, very few people in San Francisco spoke Japanese.

Now I was all alone in a small, dark room. I did not know what to do. I was very tired, though, so I just went to sleep.

In the beginning, I could not find work. I found my friends from Japan and borrowed money from them. That way, I could buy food and stay at the rooming house on Golden Gate Avenue. I knew that I had to find a job quickly.

Most of all, I had to stick to my dream of going to school.

After a few hard weeks, I found a job cleaning windows. I slowly started to pay back my friends. Then, at last, I began to study English. I had been in America for nearly two years.

The English lessons were very difficult for me. I had to learn the alphabet, which looked nothing like Japanese writing. And the sounds were very different. I could not always say the words that the teacher taught me.

I studied hard because I had to learn some English before I could get more of an education.

Some people who came with me from Japan worked on farms. Others washed dishes, cleaned streets, or worked as delivery people. Whatever we did, we worked hard, and we took whatever pay we could get. Finding a job was not easy for someone who didn't speak English. But we kept trying, because we believed our dreams might come true in America.

After six months, the lessons took hold, and I learned a little English. After that, I was able to get a better job. My new job was cooking and cleaning house for an American family named Harris. I was also able to start school. I moved to another rooming house so that I could be close to the school and my new job.

The Harrises paid me about three dollars a week. In the morning, I made breakfast and cleaned the kitchen. At first, I didn't know what to do in an American house. All I had ever used for eating were chopsticks. The Harrises' forks, knives, and spoons confused me. It took me a while to understand American customs.

After working for the Harrises for six months, I was finally able to start making my dream come true.

In the afternoons, I went to school.

After school, I went back to the Harris household to make dinner and do more cleaning. Sometimes, the Harrises sent me home with left-overs. When they didn't, I usually had to skip dinner. On those nights, I just went back to my rooming house on Market Street and slept in my lonely room, hungry. I wondered more and more if I should have ever left Japan.

One evening, I just sat in bed after a long day. I was tired and hungry. I had saved about six dollars in two years. My English still was not very good. I wanted to go back to Japan. But I would be ashamed to return without doing what I had come to America to do.

When I thought about my life in Niigata, though, I knew I had no chance of getting a good education there. I would be stuck on my family's little farm for the rest of my life if I went back.

Of course, compared with some of my friends' lives, my life wasn't so bad. One friend, who worked on a farm in Fresno, died from hunger and sickness. Another friend delivered the Japanese newspaper in San Francisco, but he had to live at the newspaper office and he didn't get paid. At least my job was safe and the Harris family was kind to me. I decided to stay a little longer.

The Harrises helped me with my studies whenever they could. My English improved. And I was enjoying school.

By 1900, wonderful, new things were starting to happen. I was able to get a job as a cook and waiter in a restaurant for ten dollars a week. That year, I also met a woman from Japan named Shizuko, who became my wife.

As it turned out, Shizuko and I moved into the Harrises' house. She cooked and cleaned so that we could live there for free. The Harrises were very kind to her too.

Shizuko and I had three children. As they grew older, Shizuko and I decided to move to an apartment of our own. We said a sad good-bye to the Harrises. "You are like a son to me," Mr. Harris said as I shook his hand. "Good luck to you and your family."

On that last day with the Harrises, I think we all wanted to cry.

Even though we stayed in California, Shizuko and I were not American citizens. Back in our day, it was against the United States law for a Japanese person to become a citizen. But our children were American citizens because they had been born here. Our children all went to school. Their English was excellent.

Over the years, I never made it back to Japan. Shizuko and I raised our family in California when very few Japanese people lived here. During this time, it was often hard to be Japanese in America. We heard stories about fighting between some Americans and people from Japan. There were times when people died in these fights.

However, our family was able to stay safe from this fighting. Shizuko and I were thankful for this, and we did everything we could to make sure that our children had good lives.

Sometimes, I wonder what my life would have been like if I had never left Japan. I imagine I would have worked on my family's farm. Life there would have not been so bad, I suppose.

There were times when I have felt like a failure because I never returned to my family in Niigata. Although I learned to speak English pretty well, I never finished school.

When I think about my life in California, though, I realize that perhaps it is better that I did not go back to Japan. Parts of my dream did come true. I did go to school for a time. I found some good jobs. My children got the education I wanted them to have. Even when bad times later came for the Japanese in America, I knew we were here to stay.

When I was a boy, Japanese people came to America hoping for a better life than we had in our homeland. We all worked very hard. I was luckier than some of the others.

As I write this, I am an old man.

It all happened a long, long time ago. But I still remember when America was only a dream for me.

Responding

Think About the Selection

1. What is Jiro Akamine's dream?
2. Akamine sometimes thinks he was a failure. Do you think he was? Why or why not?
3. In one sentence, tell what you think this story was about.

Story Structure/Summarizing

Copy this map. Complete it by adding the setting, main character, problem, and resolution.

STORY TITLE
America: A Dream

SETTING
?

CHARACTER
?

PROBLEM
?

RESOLUTION
?